To J.M.F.

ARTHUR WILLIAM BROWN vs. CLARENCE BUDINGTON KELLAND

A.W.B. *Give me a break, Bud. Put some glamorous situations in this story.*

C.B.K. *Listen! Why the Hell don't you write my stories yourself?*

FACES & FACTS

BY AND ABOUT

26

CONTEMPORARY ARTISTS

WITH AN INTRODUCTION BY

JAMES MONTGOMERY FLAGG

&

BIOGRAPHIES BY

WILLIS BIRCHMAN

Essay Index Reprint Series

BOOKS FOR LIBRARIES PRESS

FREEPORT, NEW YORK

First published 1937
Reprinted 1968

Reprinted from a copy in the collections of
The Brooklyn Public Library

LIBRARY OF CONGRESS CATALOG CARD NUMBER:
68-25600

PRINTED IN THE UNITED STATES OF AMERICA

CONTENTS

A drop of ink . . . makes millions think!

BYRON

ACKNOWLEDGMENTS

All but two of the artists' portraits in this book are self-drawn. The frontispiece is by Russell Patterson and the dedication-page drawing is James Montgomery Flagg's intimate self-portrait. The author gratefully acknowledges his debt to the artists for their "faces." They reveal so much that the "facts" are purposely brief.

W.B.

November, 1937
New Haven, Conn.

INTRODUCTION

Our name for ourselves is Artists. The rest of America calls us other things—The great State of New York calls us "unincorporated business" and denies ours is a profession—ignoring fact and Webster's dictionary.

Anyone leading a precarious life like a swinger on trapezes calls him or herself "Artist"—actors calls themselves artists—barbers, dressmakers—hordes of people blithely annex our name. It is flattering but confusing. Business men imagine we are pansies. Unless they hear that an artist makes a good income—then he is confused but deferential—and asks us to dinner. And we laugh and don't go. We probably have better dinners ourselves. Certainly better company.

An artist in America is allowed to do one thing. *Only* one, me lad! Take for instance John La Gatta—he does ladies backs beautifully so he has to keep on, always doing backs—they won't believe he can do fronts—They give the fronts to Russell Patterson. He's a front artist. That's how it works—It's all very confusing and confining and slightly sad.

There is one compensation to us altruists. We get tons of letters each year from a Boy of Fifteen who wants to be told how to become an artist and he encloses samples of his drawings which are horrible little Gauguin things. Our compensation—our one ray of vicarious joy comes to us, it is the knowledge that HE will never never become an artist—

J.M.F.

September 14, 1937
New York, N.Y.

PETER ARNO

Peter Arno

is a peculiar but likeable chap, six feet tall, handsome, and arrogant. He is more apt to be disagreeable than pleasant but has a grand sense of humor at times. He says, "You don't do good work of this sort unless you're mad at something. For several years I wasn't mad at anything. My work suffered.... As I grew up I was annoyed by things. That anger gave my stuff punch and made it live." He was born in New York City in 1902 and was educated at Hotchkiss and at Yale. His jazz band and naughty murals were once the attraction at the Bull Dog Grille. He left college in 1923 to come to New York where he provided the music for Gilda Gray's shimmy at the old Rendezvous Club. His drawings were only a side line then and his name was Curtis Arnoux Peters. His debut as Peter Arno came with the birth of the *New Yorker* in 1925. His Whoops Sisters success was as immense as their chests! Practically self-taught he has been greatly influenced by the work of Constantin Guys, French satirist of the nineteenth century. His exhibition in London created a sensation. He never answers his mail. He is a playboy, and a pugilist of questionable ability. He knows how to tell a story and can tickle the ivories in an entertaining manner. His first wife was Lois Long, the *New Yorker's "Lipstick,"* and they have a daughter. They were divorced and Arno has remarried. Of the artist Lewis Mumford once wrote, "Year after year Peter Arno has been turning out the most brilliant comic drawing that has been done since the days of the oh-so-very-different Du Maurier.... There is nobody drawing in America that I can think of ... who has shown anything like Arno's skill in sweeping a simple wash across a figure to create life and movement in the whole pattern after he has outlined its parts; and no one has dramatized so effectively the elementary battle of black and white, in a fashion that makes a face leap out of the picture like a jack-in-the-box, knocking one in the eye at the same time that the idea of the joke enters one's mind...."

PEGGY BACON

Peggy Bacon —

besides being a caricaturist is an etcher, teacher of drawing, and the author of several children's books, short stories, and satirical verse. "The Dorothy Parker of ink and crayon" was born in Ridgefield, Connecticut, on May 2, 1895, and attended Kent Place School, Summit, New Jersey. Her father and mother, both artists, met while studying at the Art Students League, and here Peggy Bacon met Alexander Brook. They were married in 1920 and have two children, Belinda and Sandy. The latter has already some claim to fame as his portrait, painted by his father, now hangs in the Metropolitan. Belinda will soon enter the Art Students League to carry on the family tradition. Peggy Bacon received her training under John Sloan, Kenneth Hayes Miller, and George Bellows, and later at the New York School of Fine Arts. Her thumbnail essays that accompany her caricatures are more deadly than a cobra. She has taken off the heads of many celebrities but, wonder of wonders, is not too proud to take off her own. She also wrote the following to go with it, "Pinhead, parsimoniously covered with thin, dark hair, on a short, dumpy body, small features, prominent nose, chipmunk teeth and no chin, conveying the sharp, weak look of a little rodent. Absent-minded eyes. Prim, critical mouth. Personality lifeless, retiring, snippy." What woman but Peggy Bacon would permit that to appear in print? Once she took her children to an exhibition of her work and a curious old lady approached them and asked, "And whose little children are you?" Belinda was the spokesman. "My mother is Peggy Bacon. My father is Alexander Brook. My brother is Sandy Brook. I am Belinda Brook—and we're all artists." That just about takes in everything except to say that Peggy Bacon is also a cat-caller!

McCLELLAND BARCLAY

McClelland Barclay

McClelland Barclay

was born in St. Louis, Missouri, forty-six years ago. When he was seven he had an experience he will never forget—he met Mark Twain, and with the great man's features indelibly stamped on his mind he painted a portrait in oil that looked like the humorist. At school he spent most of his time drawing caricatures of the teachers, and making plaster busts. To this day he feels that his sculpturing and marine painting are far more successful than his illustrations. Don't be surprised if, when the time comes for him to cease earning a living, his retirement finds him blossoming forth as one of the greatest marine artists of all times. He loves the sea and enjoys painting it. He has shipped before the mast on a Gloucester mackerel schooner and has served three years with the U. S. Bureau of Fisheries for firsthand experience. He has had good sound art training. He became an advertising illustrator in order to make enough money to get married. The girl with the Fisher Body, a series of ads that ran for nine years, made a lot of money and a reputation for McClelland Barclay. He married the model but they were later divorced. He is as far from the Bohemian artist as a high-pressure salesman of concrete mixers. He doesn't smoke, drink, or play bridge because he doesn't want to and because he gets his fun in other ways. He loves to box and frequently puts on the gloves with Arthur Donovan, noted referee and boxing coach at the New York Athletic Club. Arthur will tell you that Mac gives him a better argument with the gloves than most prize fighters. He is a strong swimmer, plays a fast game of tennis, and rides horseback. When he is not roughing it in the woods he goes to a lonely island off the coast of Maine and there the painter of permanent waves paints the rolling, unruly waves.

RALPH BARTON

was the *New Yorker's* most powerful satirist until his death in 1931.
Practically lone-handed he revived and popularized caricature in
America in the early 1920's and his drawings for *Droll Stories, Gentle-
men Prefer Blondes,* and *God's Country* placed him in the front rank of
modern book illustrators. He was born in Kansas City, Missouri,
of school-teaching parents. After selling *Puck* some drawings by mail
he came to New York, took a studio in the Lincoln Arcade with
Actor William Powell, and they starved together! During the war
he enlisted because he thought he could set up a studio in a tank and
send back firsthand drawings to the magazines. In 1922 a new use
for caricature was found by Barton when he made a curtain for the
Chauve-Souris, which showed 150 first-nighters. He received only five
hundred dollars for it but it made him famous. Although practically
self-taught, he admired the works of Aubrey Beardsley, Max Beerbohm, and Rubens. He commuted from New York to Paris as often
as a New Yorker uses the subway, became an ardent Francophile, and
received the Legion of Honor in 1927. He had a fine library and *read* the
books; quite understandably Anatole France was his favorite author.
He was a clotheshorse, a great mimic and punster, and an egomaniac
with a high-strung and sarcastic disposition that would put Whistler
to shame. Once he said he had caricatured everyone living and was
waiting for new subjects to be born. His weakness was women and
women's weakness was he. The dark and mysterious Valeska Surratt
was his first crush and always his type. He was married four times and
had two daughters. When the eldest took the veil he remarked, "My
daughter became the bride of Christ yesterday—that makes me his
father-in-law." At forty, bored with success and insane, he typed his
own "obit" and sent a bullet through his head, bringing an end to
one of the wittiest, most original minds this generation has known.

MAX BEERBOHM

"MY CRAVING FOR KNIGHTHOOD"

I: to Sir F. C. Gould

"Tell me frankly: is one born,
or can one *become,* amiable ?"

A self-caricature by Max and on the right, Sir F. C. Gould.

Max

is the spirit of caricature and as much a British institution as an afternoon tea. He was born in London in 1872 and at the age of fifteen had
fond hopes of becoming a lawyer. At Charterhouse and Oxford, where
he was educated, he quickly gained a reputation for his versatility and
wit. Will Rothenstein introduced him to Aubrey Beardsley, then art
editor of the *Savoy*, and thereafter Max became a regular contributor to
this and other famous magazines of the Nineties. He made his debut as
a parodist of genius in the *Yellow Book*. In 1898 he visited America
briefly, returning to succeed G.B.S. as dramatic critic of the *Saturday
Review*. At the end of Shaw's valedictory he made one of the few com-
plimentary remarks of his life when he called Our Subject "the in-
comparable Max." After twelve critical years Max stopped meeting
Thursday dead lines, which he had always feared, and became a free
lance. Without art training, he has laboriously taught himself. He draws
entirely from memory as did Carlo Pellegrini (Ape), his predecessor and
idol. Of himself, Max once wrote, "My gifts are small. I've used them
well and discreetly, never straining them, and the result is that I've made
a charming little reputation." Bohun Lynch, in his book *Max Beerbohm
in Perspective,* wrote, "Over and over again critics have solemnly de-
clared there is no malice in Max—quite as though malice in a satirist
were an unpardonable sin. There is malice in all of us: and Max fights,
not with a blunted sabre (for he is seldom rude) but with a foil—from
the point of which he has, now and again, snicked off the button. There
is nothing assertive or pushing about Max, even when he is most ego-
tistic. He is quiet always and delicate. He has insinuated himself into his
present position without the use of his elbows." In 1910 Max took a
wife, an American actress from Memphis, Tennessee, and since then
has lived at a villa in Rapallo, Italy. Here amid blue skies he thinks
the more.

GEORGE BIDDLE

George Biddle

has had a hard time living down his name. For years art critics have referred to him as a member of the Biddle family and have treated his work with the suspicion accorded debutantes who sing at night clubs. The truth of the matter is that the artist would rather paint a colored wench than a social registerite. He was born in Philadelphia in 1885 and unlike most artists showed no unusual aptitude for art until he was a matured man. He lays this to the fact that he spent thirteen years in a New England boarding school, college, and law school, all of which retarded and almost completely frustrated a normal craving and curi-osity for life. At sixteen and twenty-six he suffered nervous breakdowns and spent time recuperating in California, Texas, and Mexico. He fell in love with the rich and colorful Mexican life and became art-conscious for the first time. The legal career began to look less inviting, and after passing the bar exams at twenty-six, he decided to make the change. The next four years were spent studying art in Philadelphia, Paris, and Munich, copying the works of Goya, Velázquez, Rubens, and Degas. When the war broke out Biddle enlisted, experienced all the hell and drudgery of it, and was glad when it was over and he could return to painting. At this time he was thirty-four years old and decided to go to Tahiti, to escape from the past. It took the tropics to bring out new color and design in his work. He was falsely accused of aping Gauguin. He likes using people he knows as models. He would rather talk and write than paint. He knows the President rather well—they were at Groton together—and in 1933 Biddle used his influence to start the present-day art projects. He recently painted a mural in the Depart-ment of Justice Building in Washington. He is a liberal, likes Diego Rivera, and in a good-natured way hates to be outdone, whether at tennis or matrimony. He has been married three times and has a son.

ARTHUR WILLIAM BROWN

ARTHUR WILLIAM BROWN—

comes from Hamilton, Ontario, where he was born fifty-six years ago. His first position was with a newspaper, for which he received three dollars a week; since then he has earned a million dollars at his drawing board. He attended the Art Students League and studied under Walter Appleton Clarke, his idol. Later he shared a studio with F. R. Gruger, to whom he attributes the best of what he knows. His work once appeared in a magazine called *Tiddles, Toddles, Tales.* He traveled with Barnum and Bailey's Circus one season and collected material for a series of drawings that got him in the *Saturday Evening Post.* Afraid of being typed as a circus illustrator, he begged art editors for a chance to do other people. The greatest thrills in his life were when they gave him a series of O. Henry stories and Booth Tarkington's *Seventeen* to illustrate. Bud Kelland's women are his dish. He is no speed artist, and turns down two jobs for every one he does because of this. His wife, a former art-school classmate, is a dress designer of note. He has drawn Mr. Tutt for so many years in the *Post* that a baby could pose now and he could make it look like the old lawyer. All he needs is the Lincoln hat and coat. Yes, he reads the story! He works almost entirely from models—Florence Rice, Grantland's daughter, is one of his favorites. He knows how to apply "The Iron Gate." Everybody calls him Brownie and he dislikes brown as a color. He always sports a dark-blue shirt with white tie. Once he saw a heading of an article in a Sunday paper that said, "Brownie, The Dog That Talks," and was afraid to read it —thought it *might be about him.* Every winter he goes to Palm Beach with the Artists and Writers Golf Club. A sports writer reporting the tournament for his paper wrote, "Arthur William Brown does not play golf but he always wins the Sitting and Sipping Championship."

FRED COOPER

FRED COOPER
ALIAS fgc
(DRAWN ENTIRELY
FROM HEARSAY)
1937

FRED COOPER

at fifty-three remains young and observant. He can see innocent fun in almost any situation and illustrate it so that you can see it too. He can work more rapidly than anyone should. He likes music, the theatre, and good literature. He knows more useless statistics than any professor in Germany. He has traveled much since he arrived in New York in 1904 and describes a lot of things that can't be so. He was born in McMinnville, Oregon. He is married and has two children. Of his work Cooper says: "I've had no conventional art training. However, I devote much of my little spare time to study, so there's no one to blame for my output but myself." Robert E. Sherwood, the famous playwright and onetime editor of *Life,* says: "Mr. Cooper's intellect is parted in the middle. On one side of the Great Divide is the right frontal brain lobe, which is mathematical, exact, and scientific. Opposite to it is the left frontal brain lobe, which is completely cuckoo. The left frontal brain lobe might be called the production department. It is here that the ideas are born and given their first nourishment. When large enough to shift for themselves, they are permitted to swim across to the right frontal brain lobe, which is the distribution department. Here they are measured, appraised, charted, diagrammed, bundled, and delivered to the public. These two departments are absolutely opposed to each other, and would seem to be discordantly inharmonious. And yet the fact is that they're really inseparable pals. The one depends on the other. If the left frontal brain lobe were to be atrophied, and the right frontal brain lobe were compelled to operate on its own, then Mr. Cooper would be no more than an expert engineer and would probably be elected President of the United States. Whereas, if the right frontal brain lobe were thrown out of commission and only the left or production department were functioning, then Our Subject would have to be quietly put away somewhere in a room upholstered with soft pads." Meanwhile he produces the New York "Subway Sun."

DEAN CORNWELL

DEAN CORN-WELL

is a man of varied and paradoxical resources. Once a professional musician, he can always join their union and get a job as a trumpet player or drummer. As a kid, he passed an ice-cream factory to and from school. With his characteristic capacity for absorbing detail he learned the business so thoroughly that while playing the trumpet at a mountain resort, during vacation, he was half owner and chief mixer of a wholesale plant shipping several hundreds of gallons daily. His business career was short-lived, though highly profitable. He was determined to become a cartoonist, but the correspondence school in which he enrolled was prosecuted for fraudulent use of the mails. The next step was Chicago, three weeks at the Art Institute, and a job on the *Tribune* as staff artist and expert letterer. Lettering was nothing new to the boy who had made pocket money in his grade-school days by painting signs for the local butcher and baker to hang in their windows. As a staff artist, seventeen hours, seven days a week, was his schedule for several years. No hobbies except a model T Ford and a new ambition to do serious magazine illustration possessed him. After a summer's study with Harvey Dunn in Leonia, New Jersey, he wired Ray Long, then editing the *Red Book,* to send him a manuscript. Jim Flagg, "Brownie," and others wrote Long congratulating him on the newcomer. Between 1915 and 1927 he painted a thousand canvases. At thirty-five, he turned to mural painting. His first job in the Los Angeles Public Library, which was completed after six years of backbreaking work, is the largest executed by one man since Michelangelo decorated the Sistine Chapel. Dean Cornwell was born in Louisville, Kentucky, with a name the community respected and a rebellious streak in his nature. His childhood was spent avoiding school and otherwise trying zealously to live down his name. Ironically enough each year of his life has added to the prestige of this name he resented, a name peculiarly appropriate for a Dean of American Illustration. Meanwhile, he keeps up a lip on the trumpet just in case.

BRADSHAW CRANDELL

Bradshaw Crandell

Bradshaw Crandell

was born in Glens Falls, New York, on June 14, 1896. He sold magazine
subscriptions when he was thirteen so he could take a correspondence
course in drawing. Both the magazine and the art school failed and four
years later he had his first and only art training by attending night
classes at the Art Institute, while spending a summer in Chicago. He
later attended Wesleyan University but this was cut short by the United
States' entering the World War and Crandell's joining the Navy. Two
important things happened to him in 1919 — he got married, and he
saw an original pastel drawing. Recognizing this medium as the one
he wanted to use, he went to an art store, bought the materials, and with
his wife as model started to work drawing girls' heads. About three
years later Norma Shearer posed for some paintings. The artist and
model have both gone far in their respective fields since that time and
many other girls have found fame and fortune after being glorified in
Crandell's drawings. Every day brings countless letters from would-be
Cosmopolitan cover girls, and just as many from loving mothers enclos-
ing photographs and the by-line to wit: "I feel sure my daughter is just
the type you portray in your drawings." The artist takes his work seri-
ously but not himself. He does not know why anyone buys his pictures
but is nevertheless happy that they do. He still keeps his fingers crossed.
His tower studio is on the roof of one of New York's tall buildings
overlooking the East River and his home is on the crest of one of Westchester's highest hills. Why the craving for altitude no one knows. His
main interest outside of his work is his five-year-old daughter. Maybe she
will follow in her mother's footsteps and be his most beautiful model.

FLOYD M. DAVIS

is tall, dark, and handsome, an exact prototype of the sophisticated mustachioed gent he draws in his magazine illustrations. The M. stands for MacMillan. He talks like a Harvard graduate, but isn't. He was born in Chicago, Illinois, in 1896 and left school when he was sixteen to go to work for a lithograph firm, making tusche and polishing stones for three dollars a week. This was followed by engraving and newspaper work. Without benefit of formal art training, Davis has become not only a top-notch advertising artist and illustrator but also one of the best caricaturists in America today. During the World War he spent two years in the Navy. He hasn't applied for his bonus yet, but will. Although he is the best dressed of America's well-known artists he is constantly in fear of losing the title to Russell Patterson or Arthur William Brown. He makes no secret of his tailor. It is Anderson & Sheppard of London. He likes music, the theatre, good books, writing, and traveling. He once spent a year painting in North Africa. Periodically he goes abroad with his beautiful wife, and able competitor, Gladys Rockmore Davis, and after parking their two children in the south of France, they go motoring all over Europe. He has a summer retreat at Harvey Cedars, New Jersey, where he is the constable, by heck! The reason there are no arrests during the summer is that "G-Man Davis" spends his time swimming, sailing, and deep-sea fishing. Every winter he goes to Palm Beach for the Artists and Writers Golf Tournament, but spends the two weeks exposing his hairy chest to the sun and the onlookers. This brings him imperishable fame as a he-man artist!

JAMES MONTGOMERY FLAGG

James Montgomery Flagg

began his drawing career at the age of two and his first published drawing appeared in *St. Nicholas* ten years later. At fourteen, he was a staff
artist on *Life* and *Judge*. He was born sixty years ago in Pelham Manor,
Westchester County, New York. He studied at the Art Students
League, at Herkomer School in England, and under Victor Marec in
Paris. He wears tortoise-shell glasses when he works and twirls his big
black eyebrows as he talks. His mind has the speed of a roulette wheel
and his tastes are fastidious. He is openly hostile to ignorant people. His
command of the King's English is better than most writers. His frank
letters to art aspirants have avoided a flood of mediocre artists. He says
the difference between the artist and illustrator is that the latter knows
how to draw, eats three square meals a day, and can pay for them. He
works incredibly fast, in any medium, turning out about 250 pictures a
year less three months' vacation. He is an author of note, has written
a series of motion pictures and satirical comedies, and has appeared on
stage and screen. He is no Caspar Milquetoast. His caricatures, like his
illustrations, are second to none. He can cook a mess of fish balls that
would please any gourmet. He goes around the house in his pajamas
wearing a monocle. He likes models well curved, feminine, and poised.
Vivacious gals irritate his nerves, boyish gals are a crick in the thyroid,
and he says, "real men are much better than imitations in brassières."
He has been married twice and has a daughter. His father is so youthful looking at eighty-two that he is constantly mistaken for his illustrious
son. Like father, like son. O. O. McIntyre once wrote, "James Montgomery Flagg continues the Ponce de Leon among artists. Somewhere
he seems to have tapped youth's eternal fountain. At an age when many
limners have put away their drawing boards, he is doing more work
than ever before, and with a zip." At this rate Mr. Flagg will not be
applying for the Old-Age Pension!

ROBERT FOSTER

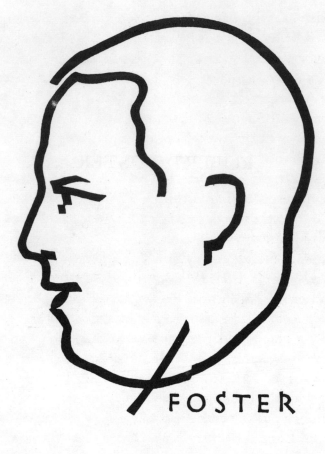

FOSTER

ROBERT FOSTER

the ponderous, who tips two twenty on anybody's scales, once taught ballroom dancing. This was before the war, during the reign of Vernon Castle, when, unlike today, you really had to know a few dance steps before venturing on a dance floor. Little Robert at that time had visions of South America and was more or less hard at work on his mechanical engineering and Spanish, and although he has been around Europe several times he has never been nearer South America than Richmond, Virginia. He had his first taste of printing ink while working on the Penn State college comic *Froth,* and his devotion to this sheet later cost him a short suspension from college. After a brief experience in naval aviation during the war he continued his engineering until 1921, when he finally took the vows of an artist, first in an art service in Philadelphia, then in an advertising agency bull pen, and later as a free lance. One dark Sunday night back in 1926 he sneaked into New York, and although he once experienced the embarrassment of having his phone disconnected for nonpayment he has managed to hang on ever since. Essentially a graphic designer, he has designed and decorated a lot of advertising, magazines, and books. But the early love for structures sometimes comes back and for some years he has been doing a little sculpture which is becoming more and more abstract. He knows personally probably more poster artists and modern sculptors living between Vienna and London than any native. For the last five years he has been giving one day a week to encouraging and discouraging budding artists at Pratt Institute. He is Graphic Consultant for the New York World's Fair, 1939.

CHARLES DANA GIBSON

C D Gibson
by MFF.

has been world famous since the "Gibson Girl" gracefully made her debut in *Life* in the 1890's. The first drawing of his that magazine accepted was a picture of a dog outside his kennel, baying at the moon, and they paid him four dollars for it. In 1918 he had earned enough money with his magical pen to buy *Life* for one million dollars. He was born in Roxbury, Massachusetts, September 14, 1867, and shortly began to cut silhouettes (shadows foretelling his future). Of his work at this time his mother wrote, "He loved birds and animals. They generally predominated in the little cuttings that fell from his scissors. The purity of thought of a subject was always dominant in everything he did." After graduating from high school he entered the Art Students League, New York. Later he spent two months studying at the Atelier Julien in Paris. When Artist Gibson met Writer Richard Harding Davis they formed a team that set the social scene of the Nineties. Davis, a clean-shaven, strong-jawed young Lochinvar, posed for the "Gibson Man." In 1895 the artist met "the girl for Gibson," pretty Irene Langhorne of Virginia, and they were married and have two children. Like the comedian who yearns to play Hamlet, Gibson wanted to discard black and white and become a painter. A few years ago, with greater determination than ever, he did several oils at his Maine estate and these with countless pen-and-inks were exhibited as a one-man show at the Academy of Arts and Letters in New York for seven months. No artist was ever more deserving of this honor. Gibson is also Honorary President of the Society of Illustrators. As a young man his God was George Du Maurier and when the two met in London, Gibson said, "I'm Charles Dana Gibson. I am an American. I draw, and you have been my master for years." Although he has never made a self-portrait he would like to claim the Flagg caricature as his own, which certainly proves something or other.

GORDON GRANT

was born in San Francisco in 1875 of Scots parents. At the age of thirteen he shipped around Cape Horn in a windjammer on his way to
attend school in Scotland. He kept a log of the voyage and in it made
his first sea drawing, a pen-and-ink sketch of the boat he was on. After
graduating from Fife Academy he apprenticed to one of the large Clyde
shipbuilding firms, but a poor business year changed all his plans and
he went to London for three years of art school. He worked for one year
on the San Francisco *Examiner* and *Chronicle* and then the *Journal* and
World in New York and was fired from each in turn for getting fresh
with the editor. In 1899 *Harper's Weekly* sent him to the Boer War as
special artist but the American public lost interest in six months so he
returned and spent the next nine years on *Puck's* staff doing general illustrating and painting marines on the side. For the last sixteen years he has
devoted almost all of his time to painting and etching. In 1927 he was
commissioned by the Navy Department to paint a portrait of *Old Ironsides*,
prints of which were sold by the thousands to raise funds for restoring the
frigate *Constitution*. He likes building ship models, writing and acting in
plays, and painting scenery. He hates unnecessary noise, crimson finger-
nails, imitative modernists, boisterous morons, and broccoli. He belongs
to more artists' clubs than there is room to mention and his work is in
the permanent collection of the Library of Congress, the New York
Public Library, and many art museums. He gets his stuff firsthand and
the thing that pleases him most is the fact that no seaman ever wrote
complaining about a technical error in his work. He fills many sketch-
books with fountain-pen drawings of heads, ships, and compositions.
When he finds himself getting a little landlubberish, he ships aboard
a square-rigger out of Frisco on one of the old-timers left in service.
Sail Ho! when next you go, Gordon Grant.

ROCKWELL KENT

Rockwell Kent

is an American in his art and an American by birth. He was born in Tarrytown, New York, in 1882 and educated at Horace Mann School and Columbia, where he studied to become an architect. His art training was received under Henri, Miller, Thayer, and Chase. He broke into print as Hogarth, Jr., and under that pseudonym he has drawn cartoons for *Vanity Fair, Life,* and other media. At twenty-six, one of his paintings was purchased by the Metropolitan Museum, the first time so youthful an American had been honored. But you can't support a wife and six children with honors and Kent was forced to turn to other means of livelihood. He taught school, dug wells, built boats, labored on a farm, worked as a carpenter and a lobsterman. Very early in life he was drawn to the sea. The pictures he painted in Newfoundland brought him sufficient notice so that when he wanted to go to Alaska he was able to incorporate himself for $5,000 by selling shares of Rockwell Kent common. After the publication of *Wilderness* (1920) he bought back the stock. Since then he has traveled to Tierra del Fuego, wrote a book about it called *Voyaging,* to Greenland, wrote *N by E,* and later, *Salamina.* He is no hothouse flower. He likes the cold climate where he has to keep working to keep warm. Maybe that explains his large output and larger variety of interests which include painting, illustrating, lithography, wood engraving, exploring, writing, photography, music, murals, lecturing, editing, and book designing. He runs a dairy farm in Au Sable Forks, New York, and works as a contractor and architect. He built his own home. Yes, he has a union card! He is of average height, muscular, has intense gray eyes and a smooth bald head that squirrels could skate on! He dislikes criticism and critics. He plays the flute very well, but drives an automobile around corners on two wheels. He attributes his being an artist and writer to being heart and soul a revolutionist. Do you want his life in a nutshell? He says, "I have only one life, and I'm going to live it as nearly as possible as I want to live it."

JOHN LA GATTA

once was told by an art editor that he couldn't draw the female figure gracefully. I don't know what became of the art editor but we all know that La Gatta has few equals today in purveying feminine pulchritude. In fact so successful is he that he owns a beautiful studio home in Port Washington, where near by on Long Island Sound is anchored a fifty-foot cruiser, and there is hardly a magazine of national repute today that doesn't carry his illustrations. He was born in 1894 in Naples, Italy, and came to this country as a boy. Although he has long since dropped any trace of an accent, he complains that just when accents are fashionable he had to lose his. He entered art school at fourteen and helped pay his tuition by selling sketches to the magazines. Years ago *Life* bought one of his cover designs and paid him $150 for it. Although he was unconscious for awhile he recovered sufficiently to make up eight more drawings and sell them. His wife posed for the paintings that started his success, yet he has never been able to put "his La Gatta Girl" on canvas. Whereas most artists will talk about themselves or their work at the drop of a beret, La Gatta dislikes to and refuses on almost every occasion. One of his greatest pleasures is designing houses and he is no amateur in this field. He likes spaghetti, boats, golf (belongs to the hole-in-one club), contract bridge, and tall girls—with a definite leaning to brunettes. He smokes, likes Strauss waltzes, and definitely dislikes swing music and flying. He hopes some day to have enough time to paint for the pure joy of painting. The only thing missing about La Gatta is some hair on the top of his cranium.

DAVID LOW

ye madde designer of the *London Evening Standard,* sits at his drawing board puffing away on a big black cigar and earns $50,000 annually. He is given a free hand by his publishers—a cherished hope never realized by most political cartoonists. Perhaps that is why Low has become a national institution. In Britain no cartoonist is quite so feared by statesmen and beloved by the public. David Low was born in Dunedin, New Zealand, in 1891 and attended Boy's High School at Christchurch. At fourteen he was employed by a local newspaper to caricature the people who took advertising space. The boy artist made quite a hit with the merchants until he sketched a butcher with a cockeye. Low learned his lesson then and there—never to ridicule a physical infirmity. In 1911 he joined the *Bulletin* in Sydney as political cartoonist and some years later went to London to work for Lord Beaverbrook. Low has followed people for miles and waited for hours to catch a firsthand glimpse of his victims. He likes to record them off guard. He says that making a caricature from a photograph is as difficult and unsatisfactory as writing a biography from *Who's Who.* He makes several sketches showing characteristic features and poses before he attempts a finished drawing. He is married and has two daughters. His favorite pastimes are the cinema and walking. He is inclined to baldness, wears a mustache and goatee, and looks like a communist. He would like to shave off the goatee but his daughters protest. Of his work he says, "There will always be individuals with interesting characteristics which invite caricature and fellows who, on seeing them, feel they have to be caricaturists."

NEYSA McMEIN

McMein.

is one of the highest-paid women artists in America today, receiving $2,500 per cover from McCall's, to whom she is under exclusive contract. She was born in Quincy, Illinois, on January 25, 1890, and left there after graduating from high school to study at the Art Institute in Chicago. For a time she tried her hand at fashion drawings and gradually came into prominence with her covers for the *Saturday Evening Post, Woman's Home Companion,* and the *Ladies' Home Journal.* During the war Neysa McMein painted fourteen war posters, staged entertainments, and lectured in France. She was the first artist to go to the White House to paint President Harding and she also did Herbert Hoover. After drawing pretty girl heads for many years she recently finished a series of America's great women including: Anne Lindbergh, Katharine Cornell, Edna St. Vincent Millay, Dorothy Thompson, Flagstad, and Helen Hayes. Although she is successful at drawing other people she has never been able to make a self-portrait, and modestly claims the drawing reproduced on the opposite page by James Montgomery Flagg is much better than anything she could do herself. In 1923 she married John Gordon Baragwanath, noted mining engineer who also writes adventure stories for the leading magazines. They have a twelve-year-old daughter, an English sheep dog, and several cats, one with twenty-eight toes. Our Subject has absolutely no sales resistance when it comes to taking on new pets. She is also an expert croquet player (Alexander Woollcott knows this only too well!) and has taken up bowling recently in a big way. At her New York studio gather the leaders in art, letters, and society, for Neysa McMein has always been as popular away from the drawing board as she has at it.

RUSSELL PATTERSON

has an inventive mind that goes on and on. His latest creation is a puppet musical show complete with scenes, music, costumes, characters, and sketches and it is meeting with such great success in New York and Hollywood that Russell has practically forsaken a magazine illustrator's life and is devoting his entire time to his "Personettes." He was born in Omaha, Nebraska, forty-three years ago and was educated in Montreal where he also worked for a French newspaper, drawing a comic strip. In 1915 he went to Chicago, worked at commercial art, and saved enough money to go abroad to study with Bonnard and Signac. He had a commission from a New York syndicate to send back fashion drawings from Paris, but he settled in Normandy and sent back what he thought was the fashion in Paris. The paper never knew the difference and the Patterson creations were probably much better anyhow. He returned to Chicago as a modernistic landscape painter but found little encouragement in this field and turned to illustrating—for *College Humor*. His slender, sophisticated, snub-nosed demoiselles became the collegian's idea of a date. When the orders started piling in Russell paid off his creditors and came to New York. He is married and has an eight-year-old daughter. For years he suffered at the sight of twisted seams in silk stockings and finally invented a garter that keeps them on the straight path. He's invented many other things but his big ambition is to architect an entire city. He is a dandy in every sense of the word and likes publicity and red heads with green eyes. He seldom wears a hat, and never worries about money. The worst thing I know about him is that he likes to judge beauty contests.

TONY SARG

became a marionetteer at the age of six when he discovered a way to feed chickens by pulling a string from his bedroom window. He was born fifty-four years ago in Guatemala and was educated in Germany. He has traveled all over Europe and America; he knows all kinds of people of all ages and nationalities—and dogs, cats, and toys and their counterparts in marionettes. Why shouldn't he know how to do any number of things and do them well? He does! And nobody ever taught him how to do these things—only the world and his own experience. His father was a German diplomat official and at thirteen Tony entered a Kadetten-anstalt and four years later won his commission as lieutenant of Hussars. An expert swordsman, he once served as special instructor to the Crown Prince and during bouts could have plucked His Royal Highness' heart! On a vacation in London he attended a marionette show given by the famed Holden and became so enthralled he decided to learn how it was done. He bribed the stage manager but couldn't see anything backstage. Finally in desperation he watched fifty performances from a front-row seat, making sketches and fathoming the guarded secrets of Holden. He resigned from the army and took a studio in London which turned out to be the Old Curiosity Shop made immortal by Charles Dickens. The rent was $400 per annum and by charging tourists sixpence to look at Little Nell's bedroom he made his expenses ten times over. He came to America, made us marionette-conscious and himself a reputation. He has six companies touring the country, three workshops in New York, a booking office, and many assistants. When Showman Tony Sarg goes barnstorming on his own it's a break for program chairmen who are looking for something different. He is a big-fisted, barrel-chested man with endless energy. He actually enjoys working! During the summer he joins Mrs. Sarg at their Nantucket retreat but it turns out to be a postman's holiday—he has a workshop there too!

OTTO SOGLOW

O. SOGLOW

O. SOGLOW

wasn't born with a silver spoon in his mouth. His mother probably at one time had some silver spoons, but at the time they were in Uncle Ben's window on First Avenue. New York in those days was rife with corruption, war was imminent, prices were high, wages were low, policemen wore helmets, and they gave you cowboy and Indian pictures with each pack of cigarettes. Amid this turmoil pictures were drawn. Soglow is now thirty-seven. When he was twelve he was too young to go to war and when he was fifteen he was too young to vote. Do you think this stopped him? Stopped him from what, you may ask. Why from working at all sorts of jobs such as packer, dishwasher, errand boy, machinist's helper, and baby-rattle painter. His education is never mentioned in polite society. But this didn't stop him from illustrating fifteen books and also having four of his own. He illustrated for almost every magazine that he never read. One afternoon in the midst of one of his creative silences he got married. Some years later he became the father of a daughter. In the meantime he was still drawing cartoons. Why, you may ask. Well Soglow figured it out this way. There were other artists who drew cartoons after they were married and became fathers so why shouldn't he. Of course the problem wasn't settled in an instant. It took years of constant contemplation and drinking. He created a character known far and wide as "The Little King." When not drawing this character he acts it. You see, Otto Soglow is also an amateur Thespian, this being his first love. So in spite of politics, wars, famines, and dust storms, nothing matters but love.

JAMES THURBER

Thurber

is forty-three years old, wears horn-rimmed spectacles, and thinks he knows how to drive an automobile. He is tall, unathletic, but can run like a deer and can hit telegraph poles with stones at incredible distances. He likes to sit around with people, drinking, and would rather talk than listen. He never forgets anything he hears, has a wonderful memory for stories, anecdotes, situations, moods. He is very good at disguising his voice on the telephone. The most important thing about Thurber is Columbus, Ohio, his birthplace. He still thinks about it a good deal and sometimes goes back there—to an Ohio State football game, or to speak at a journalism class, or to see his mother, or both. During the Peace Conference he served as a code clerk in the U.S. Embassy in Paris. Later he worked on the Paris edition of the *Chicago Tribune* and then on the *New York Post*. Since 1927 he has been a three-in-one man (artist, writer, and editor) on the *New Yorker* staff. His drawings used to be of the unconscious sort, back in 1928; but of course nobody can stay unconscious forever. He draws rapidly and profusely, all over everything. I should say twenty seconds was par for a drawing. His writing goes much slower, and he spends much more time at it and thinks more highly of it. He says his drawing "is no more than a minor nervous condition that any competent psychoanalyst ought to be able to clear up in twenty minutes." Thurber likes dogs—that is, he understands the drama of their lives. He has no dog. He was married for about seven or eight years to Althea Adams and has a daughter Rosemary, by her. They were divorced a couple of years ago, and he married Helen Wisner. There is about him something sad and vague; he is always defeated by the trivial. He had to give up wearing an overcoat because he couldn't keep the buttons on it, and once he was unable to check out of the Algonquin for a month because some of his clothes were always in the hotel laundry. He now lives happily in Litchfield, Connecticut.

JOHN VASSOS

VASSOS

was born in Rumania thirty-eight years ago and brought up in Istanbul. He got in trouble with the Turkish authorities as a twelve-year-old newspaper cartoonist and had to leave Constantinople. He served with the Gallipoli expedition under the British, later on a mine sweeper in the North Sea, and finally arrived in America at the close of the war. He is now an American citizen. He has painted scenery under Joseph Urban, has studied with Sargent and also with John Sloan. After hoboing up and down the Atlantic coast, putting on drugstore sales and week-end specials for butcher shops, he wound up in Baltimore. Here he lived on peanuts for two days and finally started a subscription to raise money for a needy artist, putting at the head of the list, John Vassos . . . $2. By the end of the first day Greek compatriots had contributed fifty-seven dollars and the needy artist was himself! With this windfall he went to Greenwich Village, became a part of the Max Bodenheim set, and wooed and married a Nordic blonde. The baby needed shoes to say nothing of an automobile and fur coat and Vassos turned out three national advertising campaigns for the cause. His drawings for *Salomé* introduced a new key in illustration and brought him into the limelight. He has done several books of his own since then. He is consultant for R.C.A. and Remington–du Pont and has designed everything from a Coca-Cola dispenser to a giant television transmitter. He has an outstanding collection of Rabelaisian stories; can imitate French, Greek, and Italian dialect but is more effective in Chinese with gestures; he likes loud ties, loud socks, and plaid shorts; his favorite working costume is an unshaven face and pajamas and his greatest relaxation is hunting. He can neither divide nor subtract (can add a little) but has from time to time been treasurer of various organizations. His conservative friends think he's a red and his red friends think he's a pink. He belongs in the category of "I don't know anything about art, but I know what I like"—and he doesn't like regimentation. Like all artists he prefers the Rubens type but when he takes a gal out it is always a thin one!

GLUYAS WILLIAMS

GLUYAS WILLIAMS

was born in San Francisco forty-nine years ago and came East when most young men were being advised to go West. At Harvard he handled the art end of the *Lampoon*. After graduating in 1911 he went to Paris to study the gentle art of wearing a smock gracefully and incidentally to learn how to draw. Back home in a year's time, he joined the editorial staff of *Youth's Companion* and later became their art editor. Since 1920 he has been free lancing. He comes to his studio on Boylston Street in downtown Boston at 8:30 A.M. and leaves before one in the afternoon. By doing this four days a week he turns out a week's supply of "Suburban Heights" for the papers. His syndicate keeps pestering him to do a Sunday page and how he evades the issue is probably what a few rivals would like to know. His work is carefully penciled, but inked in with a rapid stroke. He knows how to use one line where other artists need a dozen lines to get the same effect. He has illustrated Robert Benchley's books for so long now that he unconsciously uses the humorist's face in all his drawings, commercial and otherwise, as the typical American Sap, or as H. L. Mencken would say—Boobus Americanus. Incidentally Williams was the one who advised Benchley to try writing, while the two were at college. Nowadays when Benchley runs short of text for his book he advises the publisher to get Gluyas Williams to make more drawings. Once a book jacket read, "Even if you don't like the book, there are always the Gluyas Williams illustrations to look at." The artist is tall, modest, blue eyed, and serious faced, and has no views on anything, especially his work. His first name is pronounced "Glue-yas." He is married, has a delightful wife and two children. His only sport is sailing which he can do sitting down.

ART YOUNG

n. y. Jan, 1937

Art Young

the dean of American cartoonists, is still active and alert at seventy-one and busy drawing pictures and writing his memoirs. He is a truly indi-genous product; was born in Monroe, Wisconsin, where his father ran the general store and his mother ran his father. At nineteen he went to Chicago where he worked for a trade paper called *Nimble Nickels*. Later he came to New York, worked hard, saved his money, and went to Paris to study art for the first time. Although he once worked as staff cartoonist for the *Chicago Inter Ocean* and the *New York Journal* he pre-fers to free lance with the liberties attached. He might have been rich if he had been willing to compromise with Mammon. He likes to draw trees and devils. His devil is Capitalism. Put him in a nightgown and you've got Aristophanes, you've got Plato, Socrates, anyhow one of those humorous Greeks who tried in their day to argue and to joke and to scold their fellow men out of their ignorance and cruelty and meanness and folly. Everybody likes Art Young and at the least excuse his friends turn out to honor him with birthday parties, dinners, and celebrations. He is clean shaven, but if he let his whiskers grow he would make the kindliest-looking Santa Claus you ever saw. He likes flashy neckwear and battered old hats and cigars. He is the No. 1 citizen of Bethel, Con-necticut, replacing the late P. T. Barnum. In his book *On My Way* Art Young says of himself: "I belong with the failures—with the man who is sitting at home tonight after his day's work, who knows that his wife, his relatives and friends think: 'He is a failure.' I'm with this man and the whole army of splendid men and women who wear the ragged badge of defeat. I know that some people are successful who deserve to be, but I am with the unadaptable, the out of luck, the weary with the money struggle. I am with them not sadly, because in my vision of a new world there is going to be a different definition of success." Art Young a failure? Lord, make me a failure—like Art Young.

About the Author
WILLIS BIRCHMAN

The Author as seen by his other self.

WILLIS BIRCHMAN

is essentially a caricaturist—this book being his first venture at writing. The foundation of this work was started over two years ago and much time and effort was spent collecting the faces and facts. Birchman was born in Hartford, Connecticut, twentysix years ago and was educated in New Haven and Boston. His artistic career began when he discovered that by illustrating poems on the blackboard at school he could skip many classes. His satirical talent is inherent—his grandfather being a wellknown caricaturist back in the days when Tony Pastor's was "the theatre" in New York and he appeared on that famed stage many times with his drawing act. In 1933, accompanied by his wife, Birchman spent several months in Hollywood caricaturing the movie stars from life at the famous Sardi's. His drawings have appeared in Life, Cosmopolitan, the New York Herald Tribune, and the New Haven Register. His work is in the permanent collection of the Yale Law School. Annually he holds an exhibition of his caricatures. He is a member of the Society of Illustrators; enjoys music; plays the violin; collects first editions; drives a sevenyearold Ford; and is an idolater of Max Beerbohm.